Interlude

poems and photographs

Linda C. Folks

Interlude
© 2025 Linda C. Folks

Cover image: 978-1-998149-90-2
Cover design: Rebekah Wetmore, from a picture by the author
Editor: Andrew Wetmore
All the images are the author's, except
    the one on page 9 and the largest image on page 149.
ISBN: 978-1-988149-90-2
First edition July, 2025

Moose House Publications
2475 Perotte Road Annapolis County, NS B0S 1A0
moosehousepress.com
info@moosehousepress.com

Moose House Publications recognizes the support of the Province of Nova Scotia. We are pleased to work in partnership with the Department of Communities, Culture and Heritage to develop and promote our cultural resources for all Nova Scotians.

We live and work in Mi'kma'ki, the ancestral and unceded territory of the Mi'kmaw People. This territory is covered by the "Treaties of Peace and Friendship" which Mi'kmaw and Wolastoqiyik (Maliseet) People first signed with the British Crown in 1725. The treaties did not deal with surrender of lands and resources but in fact recognized Mi'kmaq and Wolastoqiyik (Maliseet) title and established the rules for what was to be an ongoing relationship between nations. We are all Treaty people.

To my children
Jennifer, Theresa and Patrick

The only living life is in the past and future—the present is an interlude—strange interlude in which we call on past and future to bear witness that we are living.

Eugene O'Neill

Interlude

Linda C. Folks

Aging

Shannon Bishop Photography

Linda C. Folks

This Old House

This old house creaks
under the weight of
her history
Shivers when the winter wind
blows through
her rafters

Sighs on balmy nights when
the light from glistening stars
shines through her skylight
This latest edifice added to
improve her image
a bright halo for a
withering queen

But still and all she
represents something
A remnant from a time
when stability and character
mattered
She is looked upon as
an icon representing
better times

She bears a plaque that says
"Heritage House"
She is not allowed to be
demolished

Healing is a journey, not a destination

author unknown

Journeying

She does so want
to be good at healing
Not to be skeptical or
too believing
Not to be dramatic
as if she only has a burden
To be nonchalant even
All smiles, awaiting
positive outcomes
The season helps,
though the air is
very cold, the sun is
shining through
Crocuses are blooming
in the flower beds
White, yellow, the colour
purple,
She remembers the lines
of a famous poem
"When I am old, I shall
wear purple"
"Warning" it's called
What was the warning?
Aging perhaps?
She has no desire to
wear purple
but there is an underground
desire to be more

13

Linda C. Folks

herself,
Whatever that is
Digression is her strong point
What of being good at healing?
What about that journey?
She thinks it might go well,
So many prayers,
so much encouragement,
so many taking part

She is not alone
That may be enough

No one told her that so much of life is spent being old

Carol Shields, *The Stone Diaries*

Crapshoot

What is "being old"?
Name the criteria
Numbers?
70,80,90 years?
Being feeble?
She knows feeble teenagers
That is surely sad but
none the less true
Being confused?
Well we all know that one
Being set aside to your
place on the sofa?
Closer
Wisdom?
We wish
Bad knees?
What of injured athletes?
Dementia?
Too often
Illness?
Comes at any age
Shrinkage?
Usually
Wrinkles?
Sun lovers have those early on
Toothless?
Maybe
Loneliness?

Linda C. Folks

Possible
STOP ALREADY!!
Nobody knows for sure
So just keep on keeping on
when you're old
you'll know it
Trust the process
Don't be waiting on it
Don't count
Life?
It's a crapshoot

Linda C. Folks

Cast a Light

Withdrawing, withdrawing,
desiring respite in seclusion
Days drifting, drifting, drifting on
All of life a pitiful illusion
Thinking, thinking, thinking,
dark 'til dawn
Seeming sudden, shadows cast a light
that only poignant dreaming could ignite
"it is never, ever, too late to mend"
even as the journey nears its end

Old age is no place for sissies.

Bette Davis

Hold Out

I resist, to no avail,
this coming of a new age
again and again

Baby boomers
Generation X
Millennials
Me too

The politically correct
that changes daily
leaving me adrift
in a sea of
perplexity

My body, too,
unable to fend off
the inevitable
decline
into the "golden age"

"Resistance is futile"

I smile

 and

hold out

And as to you Life, I reckon you are the leavings of many deaths,
No doubt I have died myself ten thousand times before

Walt Whitman, *Leaves of Grass*

Small Death

"I have died myself ten thousand times"
I cannot remember them all
I chose not to
I regret the choice
As some were spectacular, noisy, chaotic,
Worthy of memory if only as caution
for the next,
Others were lamentable,
love stories with sad endings
Stealing away, giving up the ghost
Why remember then?
Caution again
So what of this one?
Ten thousand and one?
Or THE one
No chaos, no noise, no sad endings,
no fear, no expectation, no remorse,
Lying down with a heavy sigh,
feeling the earth undulating,
feeling sated, ragged,
indolent
still

Linda C. Folks

Mia Tenda

Nostalgia overcomes her
A longing for her wilderness home

Shadowed in mist
a rugged cabin

An oasis
encircled by
the tallest of
trees

Hemlock
Pine
Fir, spruce

Mouldering leaves
Their scent
permeating

A wisp
of smoke from
a dying fire

The lake
Her dog

Stillness

Linda C. Folks

Refuge

These scents and scenes
slowly
slipping away

if you're brave enough to move away,
life will reward you with a new hello

Paul Cochlo

Moving

The spaces left by
things lost, sold, removed,
exchanged,
stand out in stark reality
against the old backdrop
that now seems barren,
bereft of colour, sound, and
movement
The chair she sits on is an
island in this sea
of emptiness.
An aura remains
like a shadow in
reflected light,
now there, now not.
She breathes in these small
remaining remnants
She closes her eyes,
opens them again,
and sighs
This view, this sensation
is already fading, moving,
changing,
becoming,
something new

For everything you have missed,
you have gained something.

Ralph Waldo Emerson

Something Missed

I have
missed
something
but what is it
I have
missed?
I have travelled
a long way
to get here
I am sometimes
very tired
I hold up
in quiet places
I walk through
forests
I listen
to birds
I pick up
scents
I think about
the past
all the
empty
abandoned
nests
The fireworks
at dusk
The stars

Linda C. Folks

in the night sky
Flowers
blooming
children
playing
clichés
metaphors
Where is it
hiding?
This thing
I missed
I will only
know
when
I find it
If I
find it
before
it's
too late
to
see

Linda C. Folks

The Sum of All Grief

arrives at the end
of a life
The sum of all
deaths
Siblings, husbands, friends
children
The sum of all
faculties lost
Hearing, eyesight, balance,
cognitive thinking
The sum of all hope
for recognition, inclusiveness,
new love, empathy
The sum of all pain
physical, emotional, visual
The sum of all desires
a lifetime of them
met and unmet
These and more
always present in
her mind
The sums of a lifetime

the sum of all grief

Inspired by Edgar Allan Poe's poem, 'The Bells'

Oh, the Play

Oh, the play and all the staging
set for aging, aging, aging
Director to the actors paging
come forth on stage and do your part
enable life to create art
Oh, the play and all the staging
set for aging, aging, aging
thin of hair and memory fading
frail of limb, body degrading
Oh, the play and all the staging
set for aging, aging, aging
Thoughts of life with some dejection
not ready soon for more reflection
Oh, the play and all the staging
set for aging, aging, aging
Not to be spared the day of reckoning
I fear the reapers call comes
beckoning, beckoning,
Oh, life's play and all its staging
set for aging
aging
aging

Linda C. Folks

Unearthing

Linda C. Folks

Are You There

If you only look on the surface
nothing moves here in winter
The thick ice seems dead and silent
The snow never melts
But when you walk out
you see it differently
The ice is blue or green in the places
where gases are trapped within
Deep cracks appear
forced openings from the continuing
pressure of daily tides
The ice breathes as you walk
subtle and ghostly as if it is alive
under your feet
Steam rises from the crevices
The snow crunches underfoot
There are tiny tracks made by
some animal searching for food
If you listen closely the silence
is broken by the sound of the sea's breath
or the scratching of tiny feet on the
crust of the snow
If you only look on the surface
nothing moves here in winter
but when you walk out
you see it differently.

Linda C. Folks

Here I go again

Driving down the same road
More slowly this time
I like to think
I know where the obstacles are
At least the old ones
New ones appear sometimes
Unexpected ruts made by someone
driving when the road was soft
after the spring rain
There's the sharp curve 10 km ahead
and the straightaway that comes
before
You can get really lost
on it
Driving full out
forgetting the bend is
coming up
It's always there though
That part of the road hasn't changed
for 40 years
Everyone seems to like it
that way

To celebrate the waking, wake.

Rukeyser

Arrive on time

Don't miss the orchestra
The song
The sentence
The longing
Love
Unrequited
Found
Shared
Dispersed
Family
Children
Losing
Listening
Longing
The dance
The sun
The storm
The funeral

Arrive on time

For whatever we lose(like a you or a me),
It's always our self we find in the sea

e.e. cummings

Rest in Dreams

I rest in dreams
sleep interrupted
by other lives
Sometimes drifting in the ocean
floating calmly on an endless sea
Sometimes lovers catch me out
Oh the bliss of limbs entwined
wanton and careless
unmindful of care
Nightmares too
An angry sea engulfs me
carries me away against my will
Yet somewhere in my heart I know
this too,
a temporary life
and I will be
let go

Linda C. Folks

Wassily Kandinsky
Bedroom in Aintmillerstrasse, 1909

This Room

This room is the
summation of a
long sojourn
A travelling to
distant shores
The lost Ark
never found

The artifacts are
rich with the energy
of reserve and bush
desert and barren plain
Horizons which
stretch forever
enclosing
the known and the
unknown

This small place is
a period at the end
of a long sentence

A warm enclosure
for old memories
and dreams
to reside

I've never meditated in my life. I don't practice yoga nor any religion. I'm a tourist on the realm of stillness.

Pico Iyer

Tourist

She is travelling alone in a strange province
She covers her nude body with a silk dress
and walks barefoot to the public telephone booth
Some of her old priorities are meaningless
among strangers

Reflection

Every day is
a new life
every hour
a second,
third, fourth,
chance
every second
an adventure
so minuscule
we don't
notice
like
the beating
of our hearts
and
each breath
that
we take

Linda C. Folks

Sweet is the memory of distant friends!
Like the mellow rays of the departing sun,
it falls tenderly, yet sadly, on the heart.

Washington Irving

Mellow She

With the spirits
of the season
Liquid elixirs
melt into memories
Mulling with the wine
of seasons past,
present, and
possible future
Angst away

Linda C. Folks

Peace

These woods
my sanctuary
I've learned the
language of trees
I know the names
of birds
Critters too
The sound of flowing
water
life renewing
The lake at calm
my harbour
The snow cover
in winter
renewed silence
Its gift
resilience

Seclusion

Linda C. Folks

Human Conditions

Life is the sum of all your choices.

Albert Camus

If

If it doesn't matter
then it doesn't matter
who I choose to love
above all others in this
here and now

Or that I choose a narrow path
and not get lost in magnitude

If
it doesn't matter
then it doesn't matter
that I choose to hear the canary's song
and not the vulture's groan

I can accept the fault as mine
if tears instead of smiles abound

I alone choose
to make or break
to love or hate
to share or hoard
all at my own accord

If
it doesn't matter
then it doesn't matter
that there is no special

Linda C. Folks

world beyond this present one

When all of this
is said and done

Inspired by
BISHOP ALLEN &
THE BROKEN STRING
by the rock group Bishop Allen

"Who do you need, nobody"

Nobody

You are strong
"they" say
invincible, possibly,
you can cut down trees,
split wood,
build open fires
against nighttime cold
You sit alone at supper
a self-cooked meal
with a single glass of
home-brewed wine
You count your memories
pearls on a string
smooth and white,
each one
a solitary thing
You take to your bed
awaiting your dreams
Who do you need?
Nobody

To what roads have I come walking on unknown paths!

Avijeet Das

Routes

To a stranger
she appears lost
seen struggling through
the dense underbrush of
their perceived doubt
she seems confused
out in the open
away from the protection
of supporting friends
she is vulnerable
so they thought
but unknown to them
she has a map
her course is clearly marked
a crooked line highlighted
with a black pen
her destination marked
with a red star

Crying is all right in its way while it lasts.
but you have to stop sooner or later, and
then you still have to decide what to do.

C S Lewis

Conundrum

She came on retreat to weep
For all lost causes
Hers and others
She hasn't wept for years
She takes meds
to divert chaos
Problematic
as all emotions
are equally
subdued
She could skip some
pills
This is a beautiful place
to let go
But then she might not
be able to drive home
and she might not
cry anyway

No one should live in fear.
It is not acceptable, not inevitable,
and together, we can make it stop.

Survivor's comment to SafeLives

A Woman in a War Zone

She lay quietly listening
for the latch to open
Her anxiety mounting
as each hour passed
His steak was over cooked
Nothing one could change
He threw his plate
into the garbage
He pushed her aside
and left
Her relief was short-lived
He would be drinking,
his animosity building
All his small resentments
morphing into monumental
insults
worthy of retributive justice
She should take flight,
hide
but where?
A woman in a war zone
alone in the darkness
of night

There were moments when I wanted to lie on the ground
and feel the street's concrete against my face.
Just lie down, stop

Tomasz Jedrowski

Cement

She likes to lie down
sometimes
with her cheek pressed to cold cement
uncompromising,
worn smooth on the surface
from being trod upon
by so many feet

Child abuse casts a shadow the length of a lifetime.

Herbert Ward

The Biggest Crime

The biggest crimes take
place in childhood
The innocent fall prey
to the acts and foibles
of those who
supposedly care the most
Do care for them the most
but they, too, simply
imitate postures and
ideas perpetuated on them
Guileless children exploited
terrified
or thrilled
Endless confusion
Children perceiving and accepting
false values, prejudices,
hierarchies, lack of self worth
Taught to be the future bullies,
spoilers, codependents
and shamed
And so it continues
The biggest crime
Abuse of children

We think sometimes that poverty is only being
hungry, naked and homeless.
The poverty of being unwanted, unloved and uncared for
is the greatest poverty.
We must start in our own homes to remedy this kind of poverty.

Mother Teresa

Bag Lady

I could be that bag lady
you know
the one who stands outside
your favourite Greek restaurant
and holds her hand out
and says
"change please"
as you walk through the door
and stand by the bar and order
Greek salad to go and
when you get your food
you pass by her again
on the way out
and you walk home to your studio
and sit down in front of
the TV watching
Saturday night hockey
and you eat the tomatoes first
as usual
and then you go to the fridge
and crack a beer
and
just for a second
you remember
she touched your sleeve
on the way out
"Christ" you say
"I'd better get that

Linda C. Folks

jacket cleaned first thing
Monday"
I could be her
I could be that bag lady
you know
for all you see me

Linda C. Folks

inspired by
'A Change is Gonna Come',
lyrics by Sam Cooke

Change

A change is gonna come
Is it?
Really.

You've been seeing things
have you? That make you
believe so.
Show me, I want to know
Oh we're all hoping
God only knows
But we tire of the politics,
sanguine metaphors, and no shows.
Language is changing, yes
it is,
Laws to tell you what to say,
not to say
Yes there is.
But there's always been talking
Do you think new vocabulary
will change the vibe?
Have a look around
see any signs?
I want to see the changes
for the better
I really do
I've got babes in my family
the future matters to
Maybe they'll be cause for change

Linda C. Folks

God knows their trying
 to make a difference in this crazy world
that's all lopsided

You say a change is gonna come
Is it?
Really?

No one ever predicts when or where people will rise up.

Tom Hayden

Hibernate

What can I do?
What I can't do is
elementary
Frustration
I am not a politician or
a person of power
A delegated one who
changes circumstances
Is that what
delegates do?
I can't or I don't want
to understand
Ebrahim Raisi
Isaac Herzog
Or any other combatants
willing to lay waste
I can't change the
deep despondency
proliferating among us
like another plague
And so on
and so on
What can *"I"* do?
Hibernate

It's like driving a car at night. You never see further than your headlights, but you can make the whole trip that way

E. L. Doctorow

Night View

Behind and beneath the
kaleidoscope of city lights
the homeless sleep on
cardboard mattresses and
cover themselves with
yesterday's news

I speed by their outposts
enclosed in a yellow cab
and admire the dramatic beauty
of reflected light

One can live without having survived.

Carolyn Forche

Remnant

Supplicating among them
unobserved
wallowing on concrete
who will see her
anyone?

Hunger eats the heart out
thirst fogs the brain
life a remnant

Scorn drips from
a hundred feet
shod in ignorance

Apathetic to pain
she drifts out
and away

leaving them behind

Canst thou not minister to a mind diseas'd,
Pluck from the memory a rooted sorrow,
Raze out the written troubles of the brain,
And with some sweet oblivious antidote
Cleanse the stuff'd bosom of that perilous stuff
Which weighs upon the heart?

William Shakespeare

Deny

She procrastinates
sits with her iPad
meticulously crafting jigsaw puzzles

A week's worth of dishes
pile high in the sink
dust bunnies everywhere

laundry too

The dog has to pee
OK
up for that

thank goodness

Why, why, why,
no answer

when when when
no answer

who, who, who
no answer

Celebrate?
What

This puzzle
isn't
pretty

Genetics is not about fate. It is about opportunity.

J. Craig Venter

Genes

The pathologist's heart
skips a beat as he views
a mutant cell through his
microscope
Somewhere else the donor
lifts his glass and toasts
the beautiful intangibles
of life

A train journey is the perfect blend of motion and meditation.

author unknown

Trains

The movement of the
train soothes my
supposed sapient
soul until I am lulled
into the belief that
I am returning
when I am
leaving

What whiskey will not cure; there is no cure for.

Irish proverb

Escape

There is nothing like a double vodka,
or a toke, or a pinch of coke,
to smooth out the jagged edge
To bring to mind the phantom friends

(again)

to make them mellow, all amends,
sins forgiven, every one

There is nothing like a double vodka,
or a toke, or a pinch of coke,
to make the scalpel keen
so that when it cuts her flesh

(again)

she never feels the wound

Letters are among the most significant memorial
a person can leave behind them.

Johann Wolfgang von Goethe

Preserved

Write her a letter
Let the cursive forms
seep into the paper
A message that lasts
forever,
or at least a decade

She's seen such letters,
preserved over time
in tin boxes
hidden in trunks
stored in attics
There are few attics
anymore,
or storage trunks
either, if you think
about such things

Your letter will be
preserved over time
in a wooden cigar
box
for at least a decade

Caught in memory
Unobserved

Linda C. Folks

Connecting

The options are war versus peace, and I am delighted that, so far, it appears that peaceful negotiation has won the day.

Valerie Plam

Negotiation

He is taking the artwork
She wasn't into it
She is taking the classical vinyl
He wasn't into it
She is taking the kitchen "stuff"
He doesn't cook
He is taking the bedding
She wants new
They are selling the house
Splitting the equity
She is making a down payment
on a condo
He is buying
a Harley Davidson
They have joint custody
of the dog
He will take a long ride
She will go on a retreat
He wants to punch a
hole in the wall
She wants to jump up
and down and scream
But they won't
Theirs is a civilized
negotiation

Love is a fire.
But whether it is going to warm your hearth or
burn down your house, you can never tell.

Joan Crawford

Ceasefire

Truce

We are warring
Such hostility

All the energy
fuelling our intimacy
redirected
to painful chicanery.

We take no prisoners
Nor bury our dead

Within this non-abating cyclone
love is literally dying
all our dreams
decaying.

Please

Please

Before there's
 no returning

Ceasefire

Thaw with his gentle persuasion is more powerful than Thor with his hammer. The one melts, the other breaks in pieces.

Henry David Thoreau

Thaw

She is reminded of past loves
Her own
The one suffused with romance
 bitter sweet
Days of sunshine
Little thunder
Two lives blending
then gently melting away
Ice in a crystal glass
Then on into a storm
Monsoons destroying
sacred springs
Tempestuous hours of lust
followed quickly with days
of bitterness and disdain
Blown apart
leaving only splenetic
regret
The first morphing into
gossamer dreams
The last
the last

The Todd river is an ancient river that runs through Alice Springs in the Northern Territory of Australia.

Wandering Wolf Child

On The Todd

If by some feat or miracle
I was given a day off
in the middle of the week
Would I sleep late, nestled
with you under cover of a
single cotton sheet
my front cool from the breeze
through the open window
my back hot from the exchange
of our bodies' heat
back to front

Or would I leave you as usual
and walk, not to work, but
instead follow along the dry
river bed, finding myself a cool
grass cushion under the shade
of an old wizened tree
and there take my pen and paper
and trace our body angles and
our uneven breath in phrases
floating across the page

Our unspoken wishes appearing as
small strokes and short lines
which turn eventually to a fine dust
like the ashes left after
a fire has died

Linda C. Folks

Fledge

I've gone away
It's up to you
to brave these halls
in full view
Strange is beautiful
and you're unique
Let those who know,
let them speak.
With your wounded
wings still beating
this is not the time
for retreating
Sing your song you
will be heard
Strangers will hang
on every word
Then one day they'll
be your own
flowering from those
seeds you've sown
Another stranger
just like you
will fly into
this world you grew
Hand and hand
so perfectly
will fill the gaps
left by me

Linda C. Folks

I've gone away
It's up to you
time to fledge
make your debut

Absence sharpens love, presence strengthens it.

Thomas Fuller

Absent

You are absent
from me
Off somewhere
doing something
I am here
thinking
Without you
I have time
for everything

And think not that you can direct the course of love,
for love, if it finds you worthy, directs your course.

Khalil Gibran

Searching

Many nights I search for you
I slip quietly from my tiny bed
and my spine tingles
as my bare feet touch the cold
stone floor
I grope in the darkness to find
the candle and match
I have stowed away for this occasion
The candle light flickers,
threatens to extinguish itself
Threatens to halt my progress
along the long corridor
Through the darkness, black as ink,
past the many closed doors,
searching the narrow illuminated pathway
Searching, searching
for a sign of you

The single biggest problem in communication is
the illusion that it has taken place.

George Bernard Shaw

Censored

In all the words that are written
there are never enough
to say the important thing
The truth
Everything is lost in speculation
What will he hear of what I say
Nothing
This is made clear over and over
again by the words that
come back to me
Censored

Linda C. Folks

Waiting

Are you waiting for me?
Pacing around and around
in the early morning hours
A mug of coffee
warm against your palms
Bare feet feeling the chill
of the planked floor
Are you asking
Will she come to me?
Oh, such a mystery
and is it really true
"the best is yet to be"

Linda C. Folks

The Morning After

In the sultry air, after a spring rain,
I listen for the echo of your voice

The water collecting in puddles
around my feet
reflects the light on the city streets
and I search for your image

From the train window I watch the surf
rising from the depth of the ocean
and I feel you breathing

In the moments of silence
between the waves breaking
I sense your yearning

The sound and sway of the train moving
consoles me and I take refuge in it
A brief respite from my searching
for you

The poem that started it all
Circa 1974

Ode to December Tenth

I am the carafe
Shelved for a time
Decorative but unused
Patiently waiting
for the right moment

You possess the fluid
that would fill me
The mulled wine
to touch the inner surface
with liquid warmth

Impatiently now
I wait
I am ready to decant
the essence of you

Dreams give you wings that reality cannot clip.

Anonymous

High

Caught in the agony
that is her desire

She is high

High as a kite
controlled by March winds

Soaring, soaring
above the constraints that
control their lives

she is flying

Where is he?

A fanatic is one who can't change his mind
and won't change the subject.

Winston Churchill

Creation

"I will take this mass of bone, and flesh,
and skin"
He said
"And create a woman of fine taste, a beauty
to behold
Some rearranging of her flesh, softening of the skin
with keen massage
Fired breath on cold limbs to bring response
from stagnated grey matter"
And yet,
when all was done
he cried with consternation
"It's not enough
I've done my best,
the trouble
is with
her skeleton"

Linda C. Folks

The Veteran

She is
thinking of him
the veteran

relic
of many
shooting wars

the man who is
tall enough
strong enough
erect enough
lean enough

the man with
large hands
made gentle
when
loving

the man whose
mouth thirsts
for scotch
and rum

and

Linda C. Folks

sometimes

for her

You're my pain…you're my peace.

T. Shree

Frenetic Two

Oh frenetic two
where are you?
Flown away out
into the wilderness
of blue
T'would be such
a rich sorrow
in some distant
tomorrow
to hang once again
on such
a sweet rack
of pain.

Linda C. Folks

A Letter

While you're away
I want to write you a letter
and tell you how it is
How I am keeping busy at work
and I go to the pub on Friday night
I clean house on Saturday
do laundry
I read most of Sunday
sitting up in bed
mug of coffee handy
I start over in the new week
Sometimes I go to a movie
on Wednesday night
Chick flick
I cry during the sad parts
and
I want to write you a letter,
to tell you how it is

Linda C. Folks

Days

There were the days we didn't know were numbered
We didn't count the kisses or each touch as we
passed each other in the hallway
The days when his and her clothing dried
on the line, blowing in the breeze
The grocery days waiting for a taxi
standing in the hot sun eating ice cream cones
The walks by the river on clear evenings,
the sky sprinkled with stars
We didn't count the lies nor the sighs
or thoughts about goodbyes
During those days we didn't know
were numbered

A gnome is a mythological creature and diminutive spirit. They are typically depicted as small humanoids who live underground.

Wikipedia

Beloved Gnome

Below the surface of the external
you move,
skilfully gathering treasures for me.

These you push to the surface
at appropriate moments
and I am filled with awe
at your artistry.

I poke about in this grubby
reality
searching for signs of your
being near
A keen desire to possess this
wary spirit dominates me.

But you have disappeared into your
special subterranean world
of wanton fantasy

Silence engulfs me and I wait
willingly, longingly, for the
next
eventuality

Linda C. Folks

There Again

You are a shadow
passing to the left
and behind
me, an echo heard
as I walk at night, a
light in the window
of an empty house
An old song playing
on a gramophone and
the ticking of a
grandfather
clock
There again, there
again

Behind this song is a story of a young female musician struggling
to find the space where both her voice as well as her ideas
would be respected
and not expropriated
whenever it best suited the purposes of the others.

Lori Lieberman
(singer/song writer)

Theft

You steal me bit by bit

Killing me softly like

Lieberman said

She said it best

this thing that you do

Murder is murder

Soft or not

I'm still dying

because of you

All those love words

you laid on me

All those touches

my body yielded to

When all the time

it's you, exploiting me

I need you, I need you,

I want you real

I give it away

So you'll feed me

Feed me still.

Linda C. Folks

Kinsfolk

There are two things you can run and not hide from:
God and a dysfunctional family

R. Alan Woods

Family United

Family, the familial,
which we don't as a rule
associate ourselves with, except
at a time like this when one of
our number is stopped short
on the path
This pause that causes us all
to reflect
On what? Our innate fragility?
A connection about to be broken?
Possibly the hope for something
not usually missed but the absence
of which is tested in each conscience.
Let free a mutant genetic virus always
ready to expand and plant itself in the
willing anatomy of one after the other.
Watch carefully as the members form
a huddle around the current afflicted
one, as if their surreal presence
will constitute a cure

There is a secret in our culture, and it's not that birth is painful.
It's that women are strong.

Laura Stavoe Harm

Launched

In January, 1944
the Siege of Leningrad was lifted,
Allied troops bombed Berlin,
the first Victory ship was launched,
and so was she.
Bursted out screaming, pushed by
hemorrhaging,
Stuck in the womb
they said,
Unable to float for the last month
they said
Swaddled immediately.
To ease the terror
they said
Mother overwhelmed,
packed for the bleeding,
floating away,
A blessing,
they said
Mother and child survived,
they said

Linda C. Folks

SHE
(dedicated to Adeline)

She is old and can no longer deny
the passage of time is having its effect
At night visitors stand at the end of her bed
She blinks to force them to fade
but gloating they remain
ignoble and staid

She is blessed with a family who cares
Her daughters visit every week, sons dutiful as well
Her sister wants to comfort, but with a loving heart,
dreading this quickening
of the day they are to part

Then one day, a gift, a son has ferreted to find
Poems dedicated to his mother when she was
only 17, a young woman on the brink of life
a friendship gay and fleeting
But to the young poet a
blessed aesthetic meeting

This book brought to her unexpected joy
Seventy years have passed before and yet,
this gift brings back all her years, intertwining,
a mosaic, her life, a beautiful design
laid out before her, so strong
Restored from within
Nothing gone

I don't believe an accident of birth makes people sisters or brothers. It makes them siblings, gives them mutuality of parentage. Sisterhood and brotherhood is a condition people have to work at.

Maya Angelou

Shadow Sisters

Growing up in parallel times
Faces forward
never looking side to side
and often not behind
A veil covers each reality
only guesses leak through
All wrong
Mother bereft behind the wall
tears hidden from view
To much to do, to much to do
Water flowing under the bridges
unstoppable as their life's
trajectories
Now they are old
Other known yet unknown
Siblings are passing
into the final mist
In their ending
a glimpse
A tiny rent in the tapestry
between them
A hint of shared humanity
Common DNA
The tragedy of secrets
missteps
Only snippets revealed
Who are we?
Who are we?

Linda C. Folks

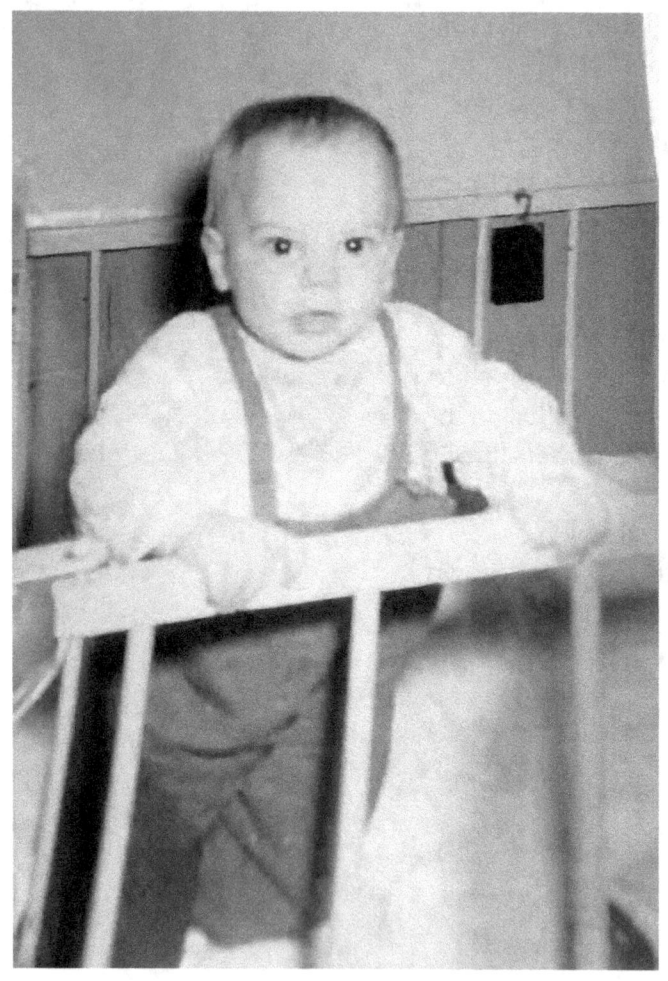

Tears Laid Waste

Decades ago in the full bloom of youth
she gave birth to a child
a son, brown eyed and fair
melancholy by nature
He needed something more
a different kind of care
Not understanding she
was filled with despair

They were alone in the world and she struggled to provide.
The rent for their roof, the money for care,
but he wanted her, no the kindly other
She held him tightly
whenever she could
but this compromise she offered
came to no good

His father had means and much more
She begged him to help her
She feared for their son
He offered a solution with considerable craft
A stay-at-home aunt
willing to play her part
and welcome this toddler
with his broken heart

Linda C. Folks

She forbade tears, angst and fears
when the decision had to be made
The father arrived with a missile in hand
she must sign away contact or no deal
"They" thought her resolute
they thought "beyond caring"
Not one understood
the remorse she was bearing

Each year on his birthday, she searched in vain
Her children called this her obsession
they grew weary of her quest
So she made it in hiding, to no avail.
How could he disappear
never to be found
Lost in the mists
like a ship run aground

After six decades of searching
came a DNA swath, it
presented a granddaughter, the offspring
of her son long lost
He wanted no part of this mother long gone
no upset to a life lived without her at hand
This, she, with true sorrow,
could well understand

Steal the Day

2000 year old myth?
Does that bring up
the hackles?
How dare she!
Does it bring about
a head shaking in
agreement?
Reactions (to me) irrelevant
to this day
Borrow the joy
steal the spirit
Have you forgotten
your renewals,
your little deaths
your rebirths
The day of the proposal
The day of your child's birth
Losing a parent
Births of grandchildren
Great-grandchildren
Life's moments when
everything changed
Experience those
joys,
those tears
Steal the spirit
of this special
Day

Precious Chaos

Seems a contradiction
unless you have in your life
a curly-headed, black-eyed,
boy
Full of energy and smiles
while building towers
or grumpily signalling his want
for TV
He lights up our world
There are few poetic metaphors
to describe how the arrival
of this small boy
could open a great-grandmother's
heart
An old woman
not missing anything in life
So she thought

Linda C. Folks

Great Granddaughter

Precious diamond
in the very rough
Who has given you
one Chromosome
over the top?
Tangled future
guaranteed
Loved beyond measure
the clichéd truth
Black, black eyes,
tiny hands and feet
Lovely smiles, held
gazes,
gentle chatter
Uncoordinated
jumps for joy
Tears
Emergencies a constant
threat
We hold you close
Tiny diamond in
the very rough

A father's love should be a shelter,
not a ghost that haunts you forever.

Osita Ibekwe

Letter to a Soldier

She should have written
long ago - she didn't
Now she writes to a dead man
"better late than never"

Dear Dad
I didn't know you were
a soldier,
In a war, yes, but
not the reality of it.
You never talked to me
Not only about your
war, but nothing else either
You were a stranger, the patriarch,
No familiarity
Rules, rules, rules,
Never spoken, how did I know
what to do, not to do,
I just knew
I've learned you were
damaged
Buried alive in the trenches,
not once, twice,
You survived, either with
help or determination,
I don't know
The damage I saw but
never understood

Linda C. Folks

The weeping, the nightmares,
The weeping you could hide,
but not the night terrors,
not the hospital committals,
not the estrangement
How could I have known you?
What could I have done?
Tell me if you will
I want to understand
how all of your withholding
benefited any one but you

I'm sorry too
Yours truly
one daughter

Linda C. Folks

Mrs. Folks

Diminutive woman

Reluctant mother

Widow

Forced through chaos
to awareness

Growing toward autonomy

Nineteenth century dignity

pitted against

twentieth century crass

Bridging the gap

Sometimes frightened

Often lonely

Branching out

Determined to do life well

Pioneer spirit

In her groove

Putting your house in order, if you can do it, is one of the most comforting activities, and the benefits of it are incalculable.

Leonard Cohen

Unravel

Who will unravel me
when I have slipped past
 this plane of
existence
into some other realm
possibly more benevolent.

Who will sort out the closets,
drawers, jewellery boxes,
giving away to dumpsters, charities,
and sometime friends

Who will read the poetry, the diaries,
view the boxes of photos, the albums,
a lifetime of stories written down
and commit all to the fire barrel
in the back garden

And who will, after having moved through
this process
with some angst, boredom, frustration,
and possible moments of shame,

know me?

As long as you can find yourself, you will never starve.

Suzanne Collins, *The Hunger Games*

Her Story

She can find herself
She knows the way
She has been hungry
Gluttonous too
Ups and downs
At family gatherings
her siblings would not
include her in their chatter
She
a pillar of salt
She stopped going
Stop!
Enough
wallowing
There were good times-
acting as a stand up comedian
in aide of good health
Her audience laughed - got well-
there were hundreds
Trekking the Little Sandy Desert-
red dust, frogs in the cistern
More,,,
Now?
She is a league of one
still
wandering in the
shadowlands

The bond that links your true family is not one of blood,
but of respect and joy in each other's life.

Richard Bach

A Message to Her World

For K, who is her anchor
For P, her kindred spirit
For H, her brother
For T & J, her love children
For P, her lost one
For H, J, & O, her grandchildren
For S, O & F, their precious propagation
For L, who understands
For some left out

Dear world
She loves you
She accepts you as you are
in all of your disguises
in all your broken places
(as you in hers)
She will never leave you
voluntarily
or angrily
She needs you
Your fidelity
Your shelter
Your council
Your energy
Your gravity
Your wonder
Your joy
You are her multi faceted planet
Her home

Linda C. Folks

Acknowledgements

My abundant gratitude goes to Anna-Marie Osburn,
without whose ongoing involvement and support
this collection never would have existed.
Special thanks to Brenda Thompson and Andrew Wetmore
at Moose House Publications,
who with their kindness, guidance, and unending patience
made this poetry collection a reality.
Last, but by no means least, my sincere gratitude to my close
and extended family who gave me so much encouragement
and support.
Love you all.

Linda C. Folks

About the author

Writing under the *nom de plume* Ellecee. Linda Carol Folks has been a poet and a story teller for over 50 years. Rarely submitting her work for publication, she chose to share on social media.

Her poems follow the trajectory of a woman's transitions throughout her lifetime. Written with empathy, compassion, humour and honesty, her poetry relates to the joy, growth, pain, and foibles present in many women's lives today.

Linda lives in the Annapolis Valley of Nova Scotia.

www.ingramcontent.com/pod-product-compliance
Lightning Source LLC
Chambersburg PA
CBHW071144120626
46546CB00006B/2123